AF471878

Printed in the United States of America
First Printing, 2019

ISBN: 978-0-359-65787-2

A.E.M. Publications

Orange Park, FL 32073

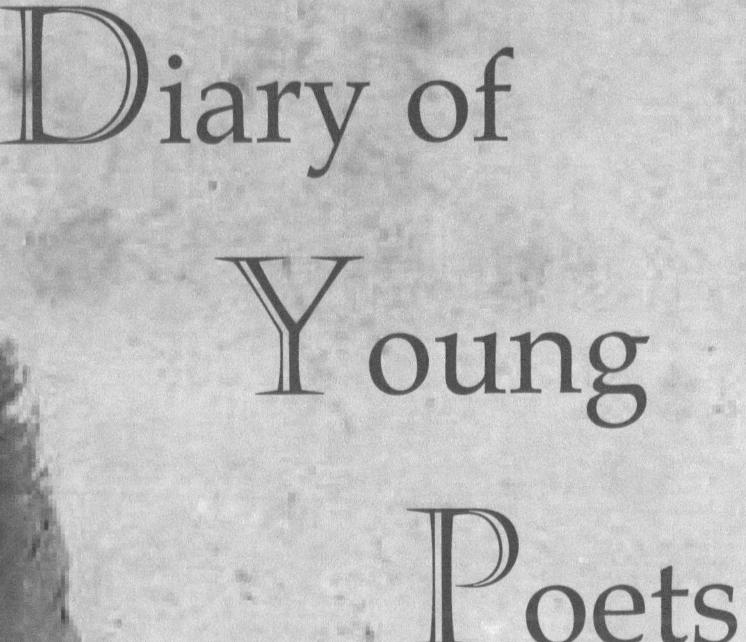

Diary of Young Poets

Written By:

The Class of 2019

(Lighthouse Christian School - Orange Park, FL)

A Young Poet's Interpretation of:

"Our Deepest Fear"

By

Marianne Williamson

"Identity"

By

Julio Noboa Polanco

Lighthouse Christian School

~ *Class of 2019* ~

Mrs. Susan Carter, Director
(LCS Campus - Orange Park, FL)

Edited By:
Ms. Jennifer Presley, English Instructor
(LCS Campus - Orange Park, FL)

TABLE OF CONTENTS

To Believe & Hope..........................9

Breakthrough...................................11

Silencing Fear.................................13

The Question...................................15

Who Am I?.................................17-18

Battle Within...................................19

Wonderfully His..........................21-22

Fears...23

Who Am I Not To Be........................25

Special Flower.............................27-28

Rule Your Own Kingdom..............29-30

We Tell Ourselves What?..............31-32

Lighthouse Christian School..............33

Scriptures to Remember...............35-46

TO BELIEVE & HOPE

We often ask ourselves…
Who am I to be great and talented?
We often find ourselves doubting
how great we can be.

The things we're able to accomplish…
we sometimes convince ourselves that we are
unable to be great by not having enough
confidence.

In order to be great, we need confidence to
believe,
strength to build ourselves up and find hope…
We need to believe in ourselves.

Without any of those things,
we have no way to become great and
successful.
We may even need a person
to help us find the right way.

- J. Brochero, (LCS, *c/o 2019)*

Philippians 4:7 (NIV)

"And the peace of God, which transcends all understanding, will guard your hearts and your minds in Christ Jesus."

BREAKTHROUGH

Often times we ask ourselves…
Who are we to be radiant?
Who am I to be gifted and brilliantly showy?

Why do I have the right to be original and
magnificent?
The answer to that question is:
Who are we NOT to be?

Dimming our light to allow others to shine
Is not our purpose.
There is no right in keeping ourselves from evolving
so that others do not feel intimidated by our person.

We were all created to shine.
By shining, we are allowing others
to share their light to everyone else around us.

Fear is our worst enemy and us…
We should not be in dismay from our presence,
we're giving ourselves a chance to grow.

- N. Brochero, (LCS, *c/o 2019)*

Isaiah 6:1 (NIV)

"In the year that King Uzziah died, I saw the Lord, high and exalted, seated on a throne; and the train of his robe filled the temple."

SILENCING FEAR

From day to day, we deal with fear.
The fright, terror and horror of being afraid…
afraid of the unknown.

Sometimes, we think too hard about
What comes next?
How big is this problem?
Is it hard?

It's time to take INITIATIVE!
INITIATIVE to overcome this fear.
Who are you not to be handsome,
gifted, mighty?

Who are we NOT to shine bright
like the sun?

- S. Leonard, (LCS, *c/o 2019)*

1 Peter 1:3 (NIV)

"Praise be to the God and Father of our Lord Jesus Christ! In his great mercy he has given us new birth into a living hope through the resurrection of Jesus Christ from the dead..."

THE QUESTION

I asked myself…
Who says that we're perfect?
Who says we have to be great?

If I could be great and alone,
Stand by myself…
I'll be the hard worker,
The positive one
And the one who motivates

Don't be afraid to be the outcast.
Don't go to "the beat of someone else's drum"
Be the one who surpasses the competition.

Don't let others feel insecure because of your success
Be the outcast!
Don't be afraid to shine.
Be the voice of the voiceless.
Don't let others be your voice.
Speak for yourself.

Be the SUCCESS!
DON'T BE AFRAID!

- J. McCoy, (LCS, *c/o 2019)*

Luke 11:9 (NIV)

"So I say to you: Ask and it will be given to you; seek and you will find; knock and the door will be opened to you."

WHO AM I?

We ask ourselves…
Who am I?
Who am I to be quite flawed,
but cannot help but to applaud—
those who have made it so far.

Actually, who are you not to be an influence
on others to change the world?
That's what I desire, though yet to be fulfilled.

I am 1 in 7.2 billion,
a mere "blip" on the horizon of all mankind…
an individual, a dreamer, a work of art.

We are meant to shine as children do.
Yet, I ask myself to find myself—
FIND ME!

Who AM I? Who?
What do I love?
From where do I come, below or above?
So many questions need answers, but thoughts are concerning.
I NEED to know…Who am I?

I am ME…a shy but powerful me.
I'm one in need of guidance
with a great aptitude for science,
One who clings to memories,
even if they are my enemy.
One of passion and dignity,
to somehow make my mark

I am nothing. So let's not be sentimental.

I am me, simple and pure.
I want to kindle the flames every lasting,
a thought ever-passing.

Within the confines of humanity,
there is just enough sanity for one to discover
the world of another.
If one dare to ask:
WHO ARE YOU?

- A. Mungin, (LCS, *c/o 2019)*

---

1 Corinthians 9:26 (NIV)

"Therefore I do not run like someone running aimlessly; I do not fight like a boxer beating the air."

BATTLE WITHIN

I find myself questioning…
Why are we always finessing the truth?

"I'm ugly!"
"I'm stupid!"
"I'll never be enough!"

We're so quick to jump…
We reaffirm the negatives
Stunting our growth.

But why?

Is it because we're scared to fly?
It's easier to lie because we are beautiful,
handsome, talented, intelligent
and more than enough

So, let's face our fears
And NOT run!

-S. Pace, (LCS, *c/o 2019)*

Romans 10:17 (NIV)

"Consequently, faith comes from hearing the message, and the message is heard through the word about Christ."

WONDERFULLY HIS

We question ourselves…
Who am I to be outspoken?
Bold, Fearless,
Unique and extravagant

Who says I can't be all these things?
How can I not break out of my shell
to stay hidden in my comfort zone…

so that no one will be offended
by how I burst with color?

We're meant to shine…
We're not to "pretty-pick" ourselves.

My intellectual thoughts will consume
those who put me down.
My individuality will inspire others to do the same.

I question myself.
Who am I to be God's child…
not letting His wonders through
the sparkle in my eyes and
the fearlessness through my smile?

Finally, we question ourselves…
Who Am I?
Finally I know…I'm HIS child!

- K. Parks, (LCS, *c/o 2019)*

Romans 10:8 (NIV)

"But what does it say? "The word is near you; it is in your mouth and in your heart," that is, the message concerning faith that we proclaim…"

FEARS

We could be…
talented, brilliant, gorgeous,
and amazing. We hide ourselves.

Our real fear is that no one will accept our light,
our brilliance…just us.
We hide ourselves
to the point we lose ourselves.

Who are you really?
You are great!
But we fear loneliness and rejection.

We should let our light shine,
brilliance show and beauty blend…
casting out our reality fears.

Who are you without the fears of reality?
You are:
Beautiful, Brilliant,
Amazing and *Bright…*
Beyond the point of measure!

-R. Putzke, (LCS, *c/o 2019)*

Genesis 1:26 (NIV)

Then God said, "Let us make mankind in our image, in our likeness, so that they may rule over the fish in the sea and the birds in the sky, over the livestock and all the wild animals, and over all the creatures that move along the ground."

<u>WHO AM I NOT TO BE...</u>

I ask myself…

Who am I not to be pretty?

I took a step back from the mirror,

Beautiful and *Free*

No worries and no fear…

Starting my life on a new page.

I'd rather be loved than be unworthy and sad.

I ask myself…

Who am I not to be pretty?

Thoughts and doubts

race through my head.

Upon approval of the world…

But that won't get me down.

I ask myself…

Who am I not to be pretty?

-A. Thomas, (LCS, *11th Grade)*

Proverbs 3:5-6 (NIV)

"Trust in the LORD with all your heart
and lean not on your own understanding;
in all your ways submit to him,
and he will make your paths straight."

SPECIAL FLOWER

We ask ourselves…
Who am I to be special?
Why should I be special,
when other people are not?

I must remind myself
that it is okay to be:
Different,
Special,
Unique

I'd rather be unseen
than shunned by everyone
or even be the same as everyone else.

I'd rather be a special flower growing by itself,
instead of a normal flower,
surrounded by other flowers
with no special qualities.

It is better to be alone
and be capable of greatness,

than to always be with others

and not be any different from them

-M. Smith, (LCS, *10th Grade)*

Exodus 14:14 (NIV)

"The LORD will fight for you; you need only to be still."

RULE YOUR OWN KINGDOM

You're not a pile of trash,
Your actually the opposite.

Never follow the restricted rules
of others within society.
You rule your own mind.
You rule your own kingdom.

Don't worry about other people
and their problems,
because they're not you.
They have to take care of themselves
before they deal with you.

NEVER give up!
Rule your own kingdom,
set your own rules.
Don't worry about other people,
they're irrelevant.
You'll become successful!

You're the King of your life.

You can become greater than anyone else.

-R. Ballinger, (LCS, *10th Grade)*

Philippians 4:8-9 (NIV)

"Finally, brothers and sisters, whatever is true, whatever is noble, whatever is right, whatever is pure, whatever is lovely, whatever is admirable—if anything is excellent or praiseworthy—think about such things. Whatever you have learned or received or heard from me, or seen in me—put it into practice. And the God of peace will be with you."

Philippians 4:13 (NIV)

"I can do all this through him who gives me strength."

WE TELL OURSELVES WHAT?

What causes us teens to struggle?
Is it fear, romance, stress…
What is the main vain or strain?

Fear grows to new heights.
It tears us apart like paper, shatters into pieces like glass and cause us to blow up like a bomb…
But you can't fall like stones.
You can't go down in shame.

You have to be
brave, strong and courageous.
You are incredible!

You have to fly high.
Fly high into the lights and
into the heavens.

Fly like an eagle.
Be eager like a falcon
and smart like an owl.

Let your courage burn bright.
Let it help you soar.
Let it burn fear.
Become sturdy like an onyx,
then let your pride burst like a phoenix
as you soar to success.

-T. Gordon, (LCS, *10th Grade)*

Jeremiah 29:11 (NIV)

"For I know the plans I have for you," declares the LORD, "plans to prosper you and not to harm you, plans to give you hope and a future."

LIGHTHOUSE CHRISTIAN SCHOOL

Lighthouse has many people.
They are funny, kind, and talented

All have their own unique style.
All impress me like a pattern on a tile.

The young ladies…
They are smart, independent, and beautiful.
The young men are handsome, strong and smart.

They all flow like a river,
a calm, soothing river.
Some flow vast,
yet others flow fast
at Lighthouse Christian School.

-T. Gordon, (LCS, *10th Grade)*

Matthew 6:25-34 (NIV)

"Therefore I tell you, do not worry about your life, what you will eat or drink; or about your body, what you will wear. Is not life more than food, and the body more than clothes? Look at the birds of the air; they do not sow or reap or store away in barns, and yet your heavenly Father feeds them. Are you not much more valuable than they? Can any one of you by worrying add a single hour to your life? ..."

SCRIPTURES TO REMEMBERS

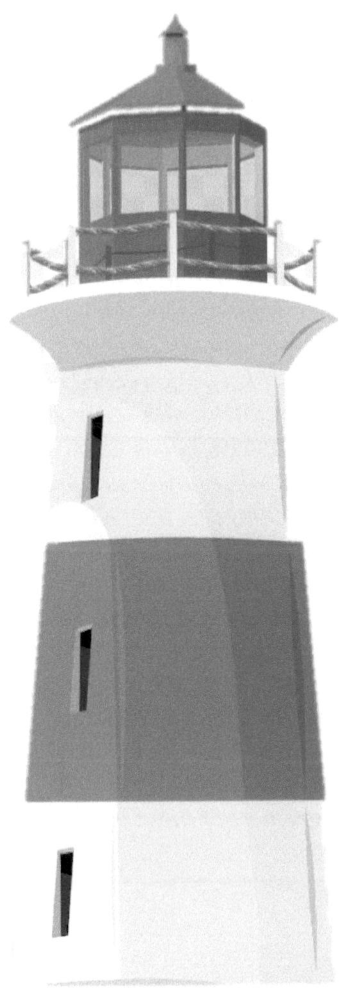

1 Corinthians 10:13 (NIV)

"If I speak in the tongues of men or of angels, but do not have love, I am only a resounding gong or a clanging cymbal. If I have the gift of prophecy and can fathom all mysteries and all knowledge, and if I have a faith that can move mountains, but do not have love, I am nothing. If I give all I possess to the poor and give over my body to hardship that I may boast but do not have love, I gain nothing

Love is patient, love is kind. It does not envy, it does not boast, it is not proud. It does not dishonor others, it is not self-seeking, it is not easily angered, it keeps no record of wrongs. Love does not delight in evil but rejoices with the truth. It always protects, always trusts, always hopes, always perseveres.

Love never fails. But where there are prophecies, they will cease; where there are tongues, they will be stilled; where there is knowledge, it will pass away. For we know in part and we prophesy in part, but when completeness comes, what is in part disappears. When I was a child, I talked like a child, I thought like a child, I reasoned like a child. When I became a man, I put the ways of childhood behind me. For now we see only a reflection as in a mirror; then we shall see face to face. Now I know in part; then I shall know fully, even as I am fully known. And now these three remain: faith, hope and love. But the greatest of these is love."

James 2:18 (NIV)

"But someone will say, "You have faith;
I have deeds."
Show me your faith without deeds, and I
will show you my faith by my deeds."

Luke 6:40 (NIV)

"The student is not above the teacher, but everyone who is fully trained will be like their teacher."

John 8:31 (NIV)

"...If you hold to my teaching, you are really my disciples."

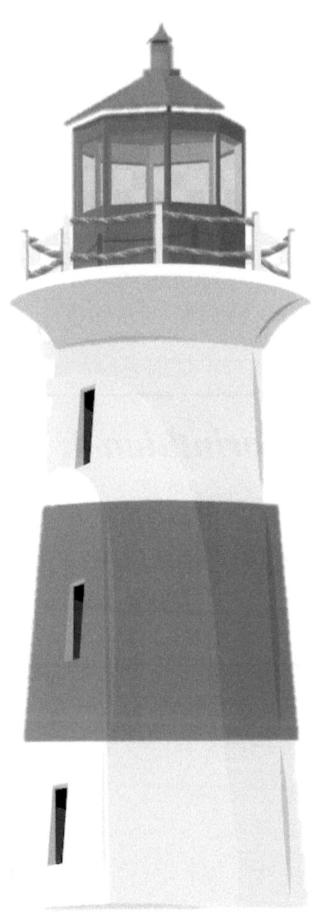

***

2 Corinthian 4:7 (NIV)

"But we have this treasure in jars of clay to show that this all-surpassing power is from God and not from us."

***

Psalm 119:105 (NIV)

"Your word is a lamp for my feet, a light on my path."

www.ingramcontent.com/pod-product-compliance
Ingram Content Group UK Ltd.
Pitfield, Milton Keynes, MK11 3LW, UK
UKHW041835200726
13854UKWH00003BA/1147